We Only ...

MW01244394

BRIAH FLEMING

PSALMS 8:3-5

DEUTERONOMY 4:19

CONTENTS

It doesn't matter where things are... The poems are pretty short...
Enjoy

If you have ever considered death being the only way to achieve happiness.
If you have ever felt unworthy of love.
If you have ever cried until you gave yourself a headache.
If you have ever wanted to sleep so badly but could not stop the madness in your head.
You're not alone. You're special. You're amazing and your potential is endless.
Sit under the moon with me

I've never experienced a warm darkness so bright
and I still don't quite understand how I receive such a familiar
essence from something so mysterious.
I seriously don't believe how free my soul is, how free it could be.
The most surprising part is that I was chosen this star, these stars,
this moon chose me.
As we flee into the galaxy time after time I try to remind myself
"stay in this moment, live in this peace.
Breathe in every ounce of this energy take back to the world some
relief.
Create happiness."
No questions are asked but so many answers are given
Does confusion even exist here? Pain? Fear?
No well-rounded I am whole
All of my suffering is under control
I can even sleep well...
I dance with the moon
I'm sure to show gratitude and appreciation
And you wouldn't believe it the moon thinks that I'm amazing
He's watched me back for many cycles, fell in love with my constant
admiration
And had to send for me.
The moon promised me that I could never be lost as long as I
followed his guiding light
And he assured me that that guiding light is always there, but we
only meet at night

Assured.
I no longer doubted the path I was taking.
After hearing the shimmer of the brightest star in the galaxy speak to my soul,
I just know

The moon sent me the most refreshing breeze as I was wading in the
night air. It brought joy
Such joy that with a smile on my face, tears slid down my cheek.
I don't know what came over me, but I felt cleansed

They didn't feel like tears.
It felt like I was recognizing all my pain and fears
and being cleansed of them.
As I stared at the moon its brightness overpowered the gloom of this
world

I've never experienced a silence so loud and I didn't understand why or how I heard so much but nothing at the same time.
I felt like I was losing my mind
But then the stars aligned
And I embraced the fact that everything will be fine.

What a phenomenal presence, or essence that is felt when unseen
I seem to feel the energy of the moon even when it is not in view

I could not see the moon but I felt him in my spirit.
I was guided.
Though I couldn't see him, he was directing me.
The stars led the way but I already knew where I was going

I felt the universe embrace me.
I think anyone who I've ever wronged forgave me in that moment of complete openness
I asked my savior to wash my soul, I prayed for forgiveness.
I'm not sure how many spirits I've damaged however I can be certain that I've healed more

Reborn.
After basking in the moon light so many nights my soul was flushed of sin and my spirit filled with hope.
I am alive

I felt the night sky fill my soul
I felt complete, I felt whole

Silently, a bright light appeared in my life with the most gentle breeze I've ever felt.
It wasn't cold but it gave me chills.
It was a feeling of relief cause it was an ungodly hot day.
I   felt   blessed.

I wanted to do flips as the night air filled my soul and lifted my spirit.
I felt overcome with a blast of energy.
I felt
I felt
I felt ready
I felt prepared to take on anything to come

A breeze that sent chills down my spine and warmed my soul
It was the freshest breath of air.
I was grateful.
I couldn't find words or actions
I just closed my eyes and took a deep breath

The calmness that overcame my body while embracing the
tranquility that lives in the night air is incomparable.
I can't explain the peace that overcame my entire being while being
graced, ever so gently by the moon.
The night sky was filled with clouds that seemed to overpower the
stars and moon yet they still shine bright
Bringing peace to my soul and joy to my life.

I was filled with warmth
I felt the root of the sensation in my spirit
And I felt it lift me to a higher vibration
I could hear it.
My frequency increased and everything that no longer served me
cease and I was at peace

Seeing that moon.
Being in the grace of the moonlight I find strength, peace, and
happiness
I absorb that beautiful energy.
I bask in the wholeness hoping to recreate the experience constantly

Staring at a night sky filled with stars in amazement.
The night sky opened as I continued to stare motionless with wide eyes taking deep breaths
The brightest star favored me and guided me to eternity.

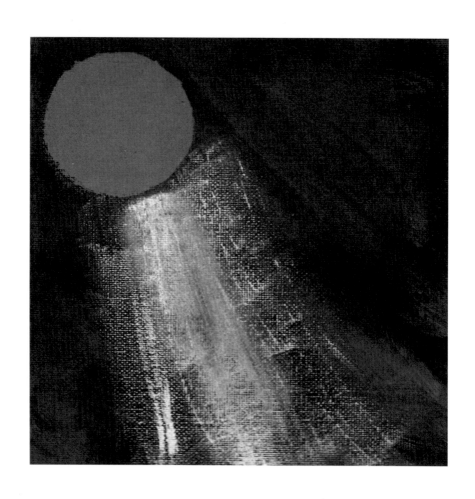

Protected
The beams of the moonlight covered my mind, body, and spirit.
Nothing could harm me in anyway
I went with pride as the stars guided me through the universe.
Clean.
A white beam of the purest white ray sent down from the moon and
cleansed my soul.
Sunday service was never this holy

As the moon lit the night sky this star filled my spirit.
This star took pity on me and guided me through the universe
This star took mercy on my soul and provided me with answers to
questions I did not know existed

I didn't feel like I had all the answers but my questions no longer existed
While basking in the glory of the moon
My mind, body, and spirit were caused to overflow with infinite peace and wisdom

It was still.
I didn't feel much but I thought so much I could barely make sense of any of it
My mind went from thought to thought to thought so quick
I was so confused
I didn't know what to do
so I just ...
Took some deep breaths around the 5th exhale I felt relieved,
Which is when the moon showed himself to me

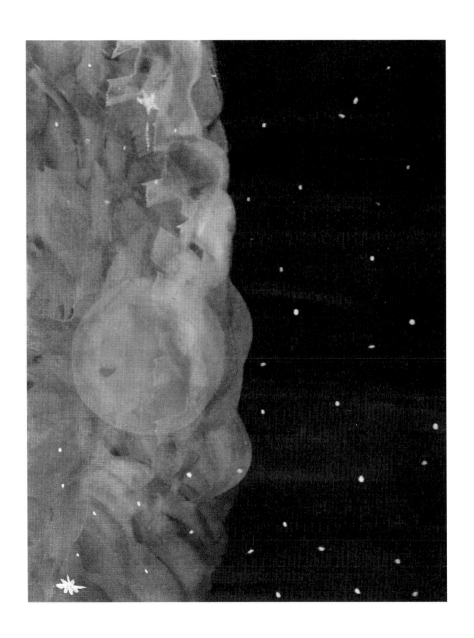

The storm had calmed but the clouds had not settled.
The beauty of the night sky was even more unfathomable than any other time
I felt...
Not lost
Not stuck
But struck with amazement as I gazed in the never-ending magnificence of that sky.
I heard the moon whisper to me and felt a star grab my hand
Now, it wasn't my intention to offend
I felt as if I was scrutinizing the night sky but I can't pretend,
I can't remember the last time I wanted to dive in head first
I didn't say anything but I felt heard and we journeyed beyond the clouds into the galaxy
I was free.

Out of the ordinary
It was actually kinda scary the way this love... comforted me.
It... I was overwhelmed. It filled my soul. I couldn't begin to explain the emotions I felt
I wept tears of joy as bliss overcame my being.
I was at peace

There is no place I can imagine I would have rather been in that moment. In any moment
Well actually no other moments existed or could exist when I am dancing with the moon.
I feel every minute, every single second.
My entire soul and being is in that moment fully
May it never end.

I never even felt alone here
It was so easy being comforted by the fact that I'm never alone while engulfed in the serenity of the universe.
My heart never hurt
My heart never longed for anyone else.
I felt complete

Time doesn't exist with the moon
I could spend ten thousand lifetimes here and each second would feel new.
Filled with peace
I try to hold on to every moment but they're all so wonderful I release each one in anticipation for the next. Thank God I am living in them

The moon has taught me many things with one of the most important lessons being patience.
Graciously, I've waited and waited and waited and when the moon arrived I was elated
But he seemed disappointed.
I didn't ask what I did wrong because I knew he knew that's what I was wondering.
He told me it hurt him that I would increase my own suffering
He read the confusion on my face and explained
I increased my own pain
I completely put my life on hold, took a break from other goals to wait or chase the sight of something when all I really need to do to achieve that feeling is breathe

The moon called me home
I knew all along I was just a guest in this place
I sometimes felt alone and saddened even with a smile on my face
But when the moon called me home you would have thought I was trying to win a race
I felt the moon call me home
I felt my spirit lift
And my energy shift
In preparation for this destination
The physical description of "home" isn't an easy one to make
But imagine finding clean water in the desert after wondering around for 40 days
Its heavenly

I'm an orange moon. Reflecting the light of the sun."
-Erykah Badu

ABOUT THE AUTHOR

I once thought I was "crazy", completely insane. I questioned myself. I questioned who I was and why I'm here. I questioned the joy I brought to others as the suffering I brought to myself increased. I questioned my life, was it really worth living?

I was diagnosed with depression, anxiety, bipolar disorder, ADHD, and insomnia my sophomore year, as if high school wasn't confusing enough. I went to different counselors and I took my medicine to the point that I grew addicted. I stayed in church. I stayed as faithful to God as I knew how but nothing seemed to soothe my suffering. Is death my only way out?

I began to skip church and research different religions for myself. I do not identify as Christian or agree with organized religion. I began to read the bible for myself, to gain my own understanding. I began building MY personal relationship with God at the same time I began nature walks, meditation and yoga. I say prayers to my God as I burn my sage. I read scriptures as I charge my crystals in the moonlight. I gained strength and became myself as a spiritual being.

I've always loved writing and I began drawing and painting at 23. I am very passionate about the mental, emotional, and spiritual liberation of people of color. My 24-year journey seems to have lasted lifetimes and its nowhere near over. I began transforming my suffering into happiness and have the desire for all living beings to achieve the same. Connect with me @BreatheWithBri on Instagram or Facebook.

Made in the USA
Columbia, SC
28 January 2019